SUPER SIMPLE ORIGAMI

ORIGAMI INSECTS

Easy & Fun Paper-Folding Projects

Anna George

Consulting Editor, Diane Craig, M.A./Reading Specialist

Super Sandcastle

An Imprint of Abdo Publishing
abdopublishing.com

abdopublishing.com

Published by Abdo Publishing, a division of ABDO, PO Box 398166, Minneapolis, Minnesota 55439.
Copyright © 2017 by Abdo Consulting Group, Inc. International copyrights reserved in all countries.
No part of this book may be reproduced in any form without written permission from the publisher.
Super SandCastle™ is a trademark and logo of Abdo Publishing.

Printed in the United States of America, North Mankato, Minnesota
102016
012017

Editor: Liz Salzmann
Content Developer: Nancy Tuminelly
Cover and Interior Design and Production: Mighty Media, Inc.
Photo Credits: iStockphoto; Mighty Media, Inc.; Shutterstock
Special Thanks to Kazuko Collins

The following manufacturers/names appearing in this book are trademarks: Elmer's® Glue-All®

Publisher's Cataloging-in-Publication Data
Names: George, Anna, author.
Title: Origami insects: easy & fun paper-folding projects / by Anna George.
Other titles: Easy & fun paper-folding projects | Easy and fun paper-folding projects
Description: Minneapolis, MN : Abdo Publishing, 2017. | Series: Super simple origami
Identifiers: LCCN 2016944711 | ISBN 9781680784497 (lib. bdg.) |
    ISBN 9781680798029 (ebook)
Subjects: LCSH: Insects in art--Juvenile literature. | Origami--Juvenile literature.
    Paper work--Juvenile literature. | Handicraft--Juvenile literature.
Classification: DDC 736/.982--dc23
LC record available at http://lccn.loc.gov/2016944711

Super SandCastle™ books are created by a team of professional educators, reading specialists, and content developers around five essential components—phonemic awareness, phonics, vocabulary, text comprehension, and fluency—to assist young readers as they develop reading skills and strategies and increase their general knowledge. All books are written, reviewed, and leveled for guided reading and early reading intervention programs for use in shared, guided, and independent reading and writing activities to support a balanced approach to literacy instruction.

CONTENTS

AMAZING ORIGAMI INSECTS

Origami is the art of folding paper. In Japanese, the word *ori* means "to fold" and *gami* means "paper." People in Japan and all around the world enjoy origami.

Do you have a favorite insect? Is it a beetle? Or maybe a butterfly? This book will show you how to make those insects and more! These super simple origami projects are great for beginners. You will learn about:

- different types of paper folds
- **symbols** used in origami **diagrams**
- types of paper that will work for origami

You'll be **amazed** at what you can make with just one sheet of paper!

BASIC FOLDS

MOUNTAIN FOLD
Fold behind to create a mountain.

VALLEY FOLD
Fold in front to create a valley.

CREASE
Fold and unfold to make a **crease**.

ORIGAMI SYMBOLS

The **symbols** below show the most common actions used in origami.

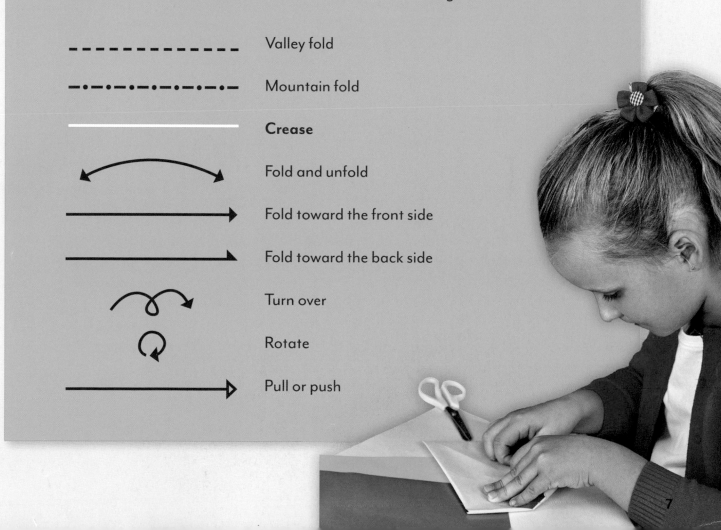

Valley fold

Mountain fold

Crease

Fold and unfold

Fold toward the front side

Fold toward the back side

Turn over

Rotate

Pull or push

SPECIAL FOLDS

INSIDE REVERSE FOLD

This fold is often used to make the head or feet of an animal.
It may seem hard at first. After you practice it will become easier.
Here are instructions to make this fold.

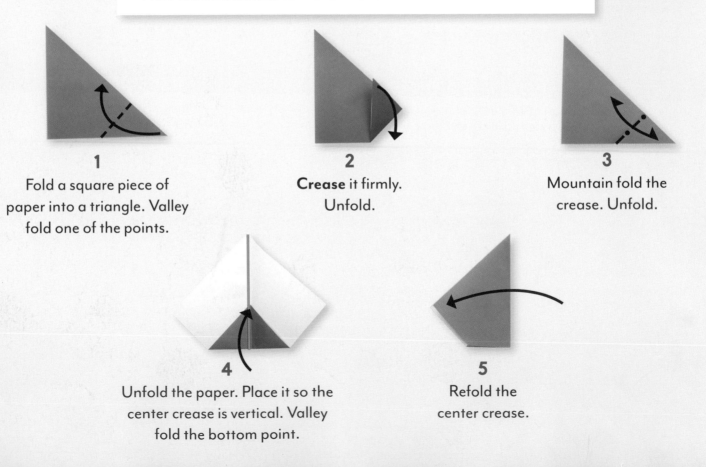

1
Fold a square piece of
paper into a triangle. Valley
fold one of the points.

2
Crease it firmly.
Unfold.

3
Mountain fold the
crease. Unfold.

4
Unfold the paper. Place it so the
center crease is vertical. Valley
fold the bottom point.

5
Refold the
center crease.

OUTSIDE REVERSE FOLD

This fold is often used to make the head of a bird or the feet of an animal. It is just like the inside **reverse** fold except the corner is folded on the outside.

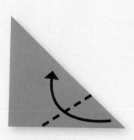

1
Fold a square piece of paper into a triangle. Valley fold one of the points.

2
Crease it firmly. Unfold.

3
Mountain fold the crease. Unfold.

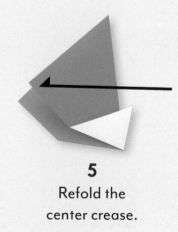

4
Unfold the paper and turn it over. Place it so the center crease is vertical. Valley fold the bottom point.

5
Refold the center crease.

BASES

These shapes are used as bases for many different origami models. Practicing these will help you improve your origami.

SQUARE BASE

1

Place the paper on the table with a straight edge at the top. Mountain fold the top to the bottom. Unfold.

2

Mountain fold the right side to the left side. Unfold.

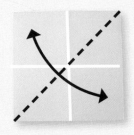

3

Valley fold one point to the opposite point. Unfold.

4

Valley fold the other two points together. Unfold.

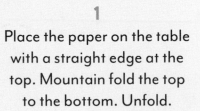

5

Pinch and lift two opposite mountain folds.

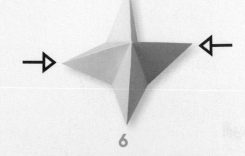

6

Press the sides together.

7

Flatten the paper into a square.

BIRD BASE

1

Start with a square base.
Place it with the open
point at the bottom.

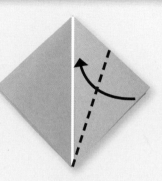

2

Valley fold the top
layer of the right point
to the center **crease**.

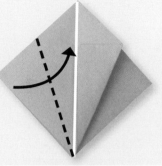

3

Valley fold the top
layer of the left point
to the center crease.

4

Valley fold the top point
down. Unfold the last
three folds you made.

5

Lift the top layer of the
bottom point. Push the sides
together. Flatten the sides.

6

Turn the model over from
side to side. Repeat steps
2 through 5.

MATERIALS

BONE FOLDER

CRAFT STICK

PAPER

You can use almost any type of paper for origami. You can get special origami paper at craft stores or online. You can also use copy paper, magazine pages, scrapbooking paper, and even gift wrap!

CREASING TOOLS

The edge of a ruler, craft stick, or bone folder can help you make good **creases** and folds.

SCISSORS

You will need scissors if you are starting with a sheet of paper that isn't square. (See page 13.)

EXTRAS

These are **optional** supplies used in this book.

- googly eyes
- glue
- markers
- chenille stems
- tape

TIPS AND TRICKS

GET SQUARE

Many origami models use a square piece of paper.
It is easy to make a rectangular piece of paper square.

1 Fold one short edge so it lines up with a long edge. **Crease** the fold.

2 Cut off the strip under the triangle.

3 Unfold the paper. Now you have a square!

1

2

3

PRACTICE MAKES PERFECT!

When folding origami models, it is important for the folds to be as **accurate** as possible. Match up the edges and corners when folding. Make firm creases. The more folds there are, the more important it is to make them exact. So get out some scrap paper and practice, practice, practice!

SILLY CICADA

- paper (square)
- googly eyes
- glue

1

Place the paper on the table with one point at the top. Your cicada will be the color of the facedown side.

2

Valley fold the bottom point to the top point.

3

Valley fold the right point to the top point.

4

Valley fold the left point to the top point. Now you have a square.

5

Fold the top layer of the right side down at an angle.

6

Fold the top layer of the left side down at an angle.

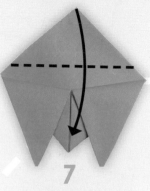

7
Valley fold the top layer of the point slightly above the side points.

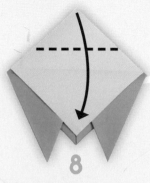

8
Valley fold the bottom layer of the point. Leave a bit of the top layer showing.

9
Mountain fold both sides so the points meet in the back.

10
Mountain fold the two upper corners.

11
Mountain fold in half. Unfold.

12
Glue on the googly eyes.

FRISKY FLY

- paper (square)
- googly eyes
- glue

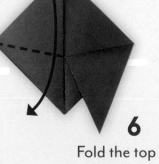

1

Place the paper on the table with one point at the top. Your fly will be the color of the facedown side.

2

Valley fold the bottom point to the top point.

3

Valley fold the right point to the top point.

4

Valley fold the left point to the top point. Now you have a square.

5

Fold the top layer of the right side down at an angle.

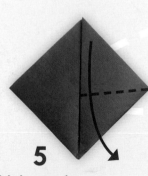

6

Fold the top layer of the left side down at an angle.

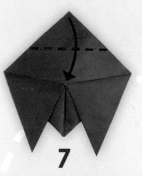

7

Valley fold the top
layer of the point so it
meets the folds.

8

Valley fold the
bottom layer of
the point. Leave
a bit of the front
layer showing.

9

Mountain fold both
sides. The points
should not quite meet
in the back.

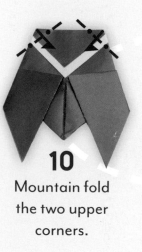

10

Mountain fold
the two upper
corners.

11

Mountain fold in
half. Unfold.

12

Glue on the
googly eyes.

CRAZY CATERPILLAR

- paper (2 colors)
- scissors
- googly eyes
- glue

1

Cut two long strips of each color of paper. All four strips should be the same size.

2

Glue the same-colored strips together to make two longer strips.

3

Place the two strips on top of each other. Valley fold the upper left corner to the right side. This triangle is the head.

4

Valley fold the top strip to the right. The side should line up with the bottom of the head.

5

Mountain fold the same strip around the back.

6

Valley fold the same strip over the front.

Continued on the next page.

SUPER SIMPLE TIP

The strips in this project are too long to fit on the page! So the ends of the strips aren't showing. Your strips should look longer than the ones pictured.

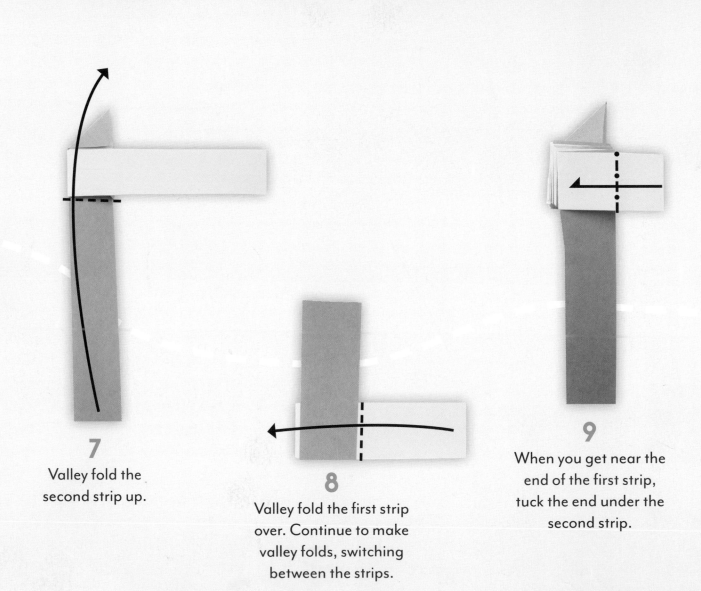

7

Valley fold the second strip up.

8

Valley fold the first strip over. Continue to make valley folds, switching between the strips.

9

When you get near the end of the first strip, tuck the end under the second strip.

10

Continue folding the second strip back and forth.

11

When you get to the end of the second strip, valley fold it into a point. This is the tail.

12

Gently pull on the ends of the caterpillar to open it slightly. Glue on the googly eyes.

LUCKY LADYBUG

- red paper (square)
- googly eyes
- glue
- marker

1

Place the paper on the table with one point at the top. The side facing down should be red.

2

Valley fold the bottom point up to the top point.

3

Valley fold in half. Unfold.

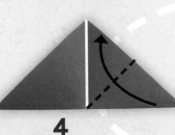

4

Valley fold the right point almost to the center **crease**.

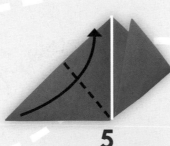

5

Valley fold the left point almost to the center crease.

6

Fold the right point into an inside **reverse** fold (see page 8).

7

Fold the left point
into an inside
reverse fold.

8

Mountain
fold the top
center point.

9

Make an inside
reverse fold on the
tip of each wing.

10

Draw the head.

11

Glue on the
googly eyes.

12

Draw spots
on the wings.

23

BEETLE BUDDY

- paper (square)
- googly eyes
- glue

1

Place the paper on the table with a straight edge at the top. Your beetle will be the color of the facedown side.

2

Valley fold the bottom to the top. Unfold.

3

Valley fold the right side to the left side. Unfold.

4

Valley fold the
right side to the
center **crease**.

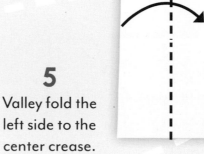

5

Valley fold the
left side to the
center crease.

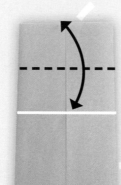

6

Valley fold the top
down to the center
crease. Unfold.

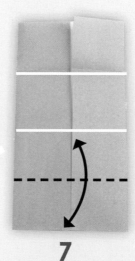

7

Valley fold the
bottom up to the
center crease.
Unfold.

Continued
on the
next page.

8

Mountain fold
the top two
corners. Unfold.

9

Open the top corners. Pull
the corners apart. Valley
fold so the top edge meets
the center **crease**.

10

Press flat.

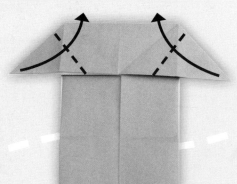

11

Valley fold the points
so they stick up above
the top edge.

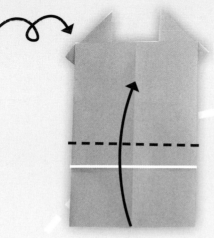

12

Turn the model over from side to side. Valley fold the bottom slightly above the lower **crease**.

13

Turn the model over from side to side. Valley fold sides to the edges of the triangles.

14

Make an inside **reverse** fold on each bottom corner (see page 8).

15

Turn the model over from side to side. Glue on the googly eyes.

BREEZY
BUTTERFLY

- paper (square)
- chenille stem
- scissors
- tape

1

Place the paper on the table with one point at the top. Your butterfly will be the color of the facedown side.

2

Valley fold bottom point to the top point. Unfold.

3

Valley fold right point to left point. Unfold.

4

Rotate the paper so a straight edge is at the top. Valley fold the bottom edge to the top edge. Unfold.

5

Valley fold the left edge to the right edge. Unfold.

6

Valley fold each
point into the center.

7

Turn the paper over
from side to side.
Valley fold each
point to the center.

8

Completely unfold
the paper. Turn it
over from side to side.

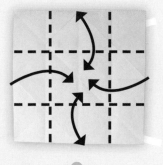

Continued
on the
next page.

9

Valley fold the top and bottom
edges of the paper to the center.
Unfold. Valley fold the right and
left edges to the center.

10

Open the top corners. Pull
the corners apart. Valley
fold so the top edge meets
the center **crease**.

11

Repeat with the
bottom corners.
Press flat.

12

Mountain fold the
top edge to the
bottom edge.

13

Valley fold the top layer of
the right point along the
center **crease**. Repeat with
the left point. The points
will meet below the bottom
edge, creating a triangle.

14

Valley fold the top
layer of the right edge
slightly. Repeat with
the left edge.

15

Valley fold the right point to the left point.

16

Rotate the model to the left so the fold is at the top. Mountain fold a thin triangle along the top left point. **Crease** well and unfold. This will form the butterfly's body.

17

Valley fold the top layer on the crease from step 16. Turn the model over from side to side. Valley fold the other layer the same way. Crease well. These are the wings.

18

Separate the wings at the crease.

19

Cut two pieces of chenille stem. Curl them into antenna shapes. Tape the ends to the back of the butterfly.

GLOSSARY

accurate — exact or correct.

amaze — to surprise or fill with wonder.

crease — 1. a line made by folding something.
2. to make a sharp line in something by folding it.

diagram — a drawing that shows how something
works or how parts go together.

optional — something you can choose, but is not required.

reverse — backwards, in the opposite direction.

symbol — an object or picture that stands for or
represents something.